Polly Pennywise Takes a Vacation

By Joanne Shaw   Illustrated by Petra Bockus

Polly Pennywise Takes a Vacation
By Joanne Shaw
ISBN 978-1-927799-13-0
Copyright 2018 All rights reserved.
No part of this work covered by the publisher's copyright may be reproduced or copied in any form or by any means without the written permission of the publisher.

**Polly Pennywise
Takes a Vacation
by
Joanne Shaw**

© 2011 Polly Pennywise Series of Children's Books

Dedication

Esther Pearl Cini (Lovingly referred to as Polly) January 24, 1926 - June 1, 2004

The Polly Pennywise series of children's books is dedicated to my mother, Polly Cini.

She lived in a world of poverty as a child. She didn't have access to a full education. She raised four children, ran a household and kept things going through tough times. Her nickname was Polly the Cook and she could make a meal out of virtually anything. I know that she would be proud to have these books named for her.

She taught me to value my education, appreciate everything that I have in life, and to love people of all cultures, religions and backgrounds.

These books are intended to be read to or by children to help them appreciate some fundamentals of money management. In addition to lessons in saving and investing money, there are other underlying lessons about life, such as grocery shopping for nutritious food, how to buy a car or take a vacation. The end of each book features a summary of helpful hints related to the book's topic. The story is presented as a dialogue between Pam and her grandmother who she fondly refers to as Nanny.

~ Joanne L. Shaw

Polly Pennywise Takes a Vacation

Little Pam was very excited. Polly Pennywise had promised they'd sit down together and plan a vacation. Pam loved to travel and she really loved her Nanny a lot so this was going to be an extra special vacation. She wondered if they'd go somewhere exotic and what she should bring with her. She went to have lunch with Polly Pennywise and plan the trip.

"Hi Nanny, how are you?"

"Oh, I'm doing fine for an old lady. How are you?"

"I'm so excited about taking a trip with you. Where do you think we should go?"

"Well, we need to talk about what we want to do and things we want to see, and then we can figure it out. But first, let's have lunch."

"Wow, and what a lunch it is! What are all these different foods, Nanny?"

"Well, I thought we'd have a Mediterranean lunch. So we have Greek salad, black olives, fresh baked bread with olive oil and balsamic vinegar in a plate for dipping, and a cheese ravioli."

"Why is this Mediterranean?"

"Well, the salad's from Greece, the baked bread with oil and balsamic vinegar is from Italy, and the ravioli is from Malta. You can get black or green olives in most Mediterranean countries."

"Wasn't Grampa from Malta?"

"Well, Grampa's family was from Malta. His father came to Canada before your Grampa was born so that he could work and bring the family to Canada. Your Grampa was actually born in downtown Toronto but he never forgot his roots."

"How can people have roots, Nanny?"

"Well, that's an expression that probably comes from the idea of the root of your family tree. Your aunt Heather does genealogy which means she studies and follows various people in a family – where they were born and married and died over time. That way she can get a picture of the complete family history and build a family tree," Polly explained. "But let's eat now and talk about our various options for taking a vacation."

"Wow, this is delicious! It must be healthy too."

"Actually, there's much less heart disease and other problems for people who eat a Mediterranean diet because it's so healthy," Polly said. "Most of the vegetables and olives are grown locally, so they're fresh and not mass-produced. That's why I like to buy my fruits and vegetables from local farmers, because with less travel time they're fresher."

"Thanks for such a great meal, Nanny," Pam said. "Now, how do we plan a vacation? Where do we start?"

"I think it's important to have the best vacation every time you go away. There are at least two ways to do that. You hop on a plane and just go somewhere, or you plan where and what and take some time to understand the people you're about to meet.

"For me, part of the fun in travelling is to understand the culture and the people of the country I'm visiting. I really like to learn more about places and their people. This is something that makes Canada so unique. We have people from all over the world right here, and we honour their cultures, languages and differences. This is the mosaic that makes up Canada. Something like this tossed salad here."

"Nanny, how can Canada be like a tossed salad?"

"You see, the whole salad works in harmony. When you take a bite, there are many different flavours involved, and that gives it the richness of taste. At the same time, each piece in the salad is an individual with its own qualities and strengths. Just look at that beautiful romaine lettuce or the white feta cheese. Each part of the salad, just like each culture in Canada, has a special trait and uniqueness. Together we all taste great! Ha-ha!"

"Nanny, you're so funny! I want to experience other cultures and people in their own country too."

"There are a number of things to consider before we decide where to go. We need to think about cost, language, customs, currency, travel time, insurance, climate and inoculation."

"That sounds really complicated, Nanny. Is this going to take a long time? Because I really want to start packing."

"Well, it's important to cover all the bases in order to maximize our time when we go away. We want to stay somewhere nice and comfortable, and we don't want to worry about having enough money to buy some local crafts when we're there. It's important to take care of our health. Many countries have different diseases so we may need to take some shots ahead of time to be safe. If we have insurance then we can get any medical care we might need while away, or even cancel our trip if we have to."

"No way am I cancelling anything!"

"Well, the purpose of insurance is to cover things that we might not expect to happen. Hopefully we never have to use it," Polly said.

"Let's start by thinking about language," she continued. "Do we want to go to a country that speaks enough English so that we can get around without needing another language? Many countries speak more than one language, like Costa Rica where the principal language is Spanish but most people also speak English. We could practice speaking some basic Spanish, but we could also speak English and therefore find out more while we're there. In Japan most people in the cities can speak English but out in the country most people only speak Japanese."

"What money will we use?" Pam asked.

"There are different currencies in different countries so we'll need to understand how to convert Canadian dollars to the local currency. In Japan they use the yen, in Mexico they use pesos, and Malta is part of the European Union so they use euros."

"More importantly," Polly continued, "we want to respect the customs of other countries. Some Middle Eastern and African countries expect women to cover their heads out of respect for the Islamic religion. Many countries have beautiful Catholic cathedrals to visit, but we must respect these holy places and wear proper clothing that won't insult the people of that faith. It's best to wear long pants and sleeves to show respect, even if it's hot. If you visit a Buddhist temple you must always remove your shoes before entering. While in these holy places you should whisper and not make a lot of noise. Often there'll be people in the cathedral or temple who are worshipping or praying and we need to respect that.

"It's also important to respect the environment. In Australia the Aboriginals consider Ayers Rock (known locally as Uluru) sacred and it should not be climbed. Unfortunately some foreigners still go there and climb Ayers Rock. This is disrespectful of the local natives of Australia.

"In the South Pacific, in places like Fiji, the coral reef is magnificent, but if you're swimming near the reefs you must be sure not to touch anything because it might upset the balance of nature. The coral reefs are one of the Earth's most precious resources because they support all kinds of life in the ocean. The same is true of the mangroves of Costa Rica.

"Finally," Polly said, "you need to know the climate for that part of the country you're visiting. Specifically, it helps to know the climate for the season when you're visiting so you know what clothing to take, and whether or not you need to worry about infections."

"Nanny, this seems like a lot to know ahead of time. How will we find all this information?"

"We really only need to completely research the country we're going to visit. The library is a good source of information and we can use technology to search online. There are specific books that can provide details about the country we're going to visit. Or we can read the *Travel* section of the newspaper. It's also very interesting to learn the history of the country. This helps us understand more about the culture and customs. We could also use a travel agent. Finally, we need to ensure that our passports are up to date, and ask our doctor if we need to be inoculated."

"What's that?"

"Well, you know how people here get a flu shot to prevent getting the flu?"

"Yes, but I don't like needles."

"I don't think that anyone likes needles, but when you travel to certain countries it's very important to get the right shots or inoculation to prevent getting local diseases. Some of these require multiple shots over a period of time so it's important to know in advance what you need."

"Anyone traveling to the Caribbean should take a series of shots to prevent hepatitis. And if you travel to Japan for more than a month and plan to visit the country areas, particularly from June to September, you'll need a series of shots to prevent encephalitis.

"These are things we can do while we're busy saving money to go on vacation. Depending on where we want to go, that may take some time. Some vacations are very expensive and require a lot of travel time. Others are shorter trips and therefore less expensive. Where you stay also determines how expensive it is.

"Many college students travel to Europe inexpensively by staying in hostels and backpacking to get around rather than renting a car. That's fine for college students but your Nanny's too old to stay in a hostel or backpack anywhere. I like my comforts when I travel. Maybe you'll travel with friends in the future when you can try the inexpensive route. There's so much to see in Europe but the countries are very close to one another so you can see many in one trip.

"This is very different from Canada where you can spend days just going from one province to another. It takes hours in a plane just to fly across Canada. We're very fortunate to have this huge country with so many natural wonders like mountains, lakes, forests and icebergs. I hope you'll travel all across Canada some day so you can appreciate just how lucky we are."

"I promise, Nanny, because I love to travel. I can go by car, train or plane and visit so many different parts of Canada and meet all kinds of different people. But I was hoping for now that we'd go someplace warm in the middle of winter just to have a break from the cold weather!"

"So you want to go somewhere warm. Well, that'll be the first priority on our vacation plan," Polly said. "There are lots of warm places. Some don't even get winter so they're warm all year round. Other places have a sort of winter but nothing like Canada's. Places like Sydney, Australia, have winter at a different time of year than us, so that when it's our summer it's their winter. Winter in Sydney might mean plus eight degrees Celsius whereas in parts of Canada it can be as cold as minus forty degrees Celsius."

"That's a big difference," Pam said. "You know it's cold when your bare fingers stick to the door knob!"

"So we want someplace warm, but what about language? Do you want to try speaking another language? There are many countries where the first language is Spanish. It's a good language to learn. People in other countries are happy when you try to speak their language. It's like a compliment, and shows that you care enough to learn some of their language. It's very difficult, almost impossible, to fully understand and appreciate another culture unless you know their language."

"Nanny, I'd like to go someplace where almost everyone speaks English so I can find my way around and ask them about their country. But I'd also like some exposure to another language. I'd like a place with lots of history too."

"Pam, I have a great idea. How about visiting the home of your ancestors? Malta! It's warm, there's lots of history, and everyone speaks English as well as Maltese. That's a unique language with three major influences – Arabic, Latin and Greek."

"Malta is perfect! It'll be warm, even during our winter. We'll only need a sweater at night. We can swim in the Mediterranean or in the hotel pool. This sounds wonderful! Where exactly is Malta?"

"It's a series of three small islands – Malta, Gozo and Comina. It's in the center of the Mediterranean Sea – north of Tunisia, and south of Italy. Historically, its position made it a very interesting place since it's a strategic location for trade, among other things.

"So, let's look at how we're going to get there and what it'll cost. We also need specific details of how to get around in Malta and where we should stay."

Pam and Polly Pennywise agreed to meet again the following week to pool the information that each of them had found out about Malta. Pam searched online for flight information, while Polly Pennywise spoke to a travel agent and visited the library.

Pam learned there was no direct flight to Malta so they'd have to fly through a major airport in Europe, either Germany's Frankfurt or England's Heathrow, both of which are major hubs for European flights. From there they'd take another flight to Malta. Their trip would take roughly 13 hours of flying, with some additional stopover time.

Polly Pennywise found a really nice hotel on the northern tip of the main island, overlooking the Mediterranean and close to the Gozo Ferry. The service and restaurants were supposed to be very good. She also found out that there was no need for vaccines or inoculation, which made Pam very happy.

Now it was time to work out the cost of their trip. The main considerations were:

- ☑ Air fare
- ☑ Hotel accommodations
- ☑ Meals
- ☑ Spending money for special exhibits, entertainment, local crafts and souvenirs
- ☑ Travel insurance

$ The airfare involved two separate trips to be booked from Canada in Canadian dollars. The total for both return flights for Polly Pennywise and Pam was $3400.

$ Although the usual room rate at the hotel was $224 per night, the sale price was currently $86 Canadian, or $602 for the week. Since this would be paid in Malta, it had to be converted to euros.

$ The cost of daily meals for two people was estimated at $100 Canadian a day, or $700 for a week.

$ For general spending money, they figured $500 Canadian.

- $ The total cash needed (not including airfare) was estimated at roughly 1800 euros. By using an online currency conversion program they determined that the Canadian dollars required to buy that amount in euros would be roughly $2700.

So the total cost of their trip would be approximately $3400 plus $2700, for a total of $6100 Canadian. Travel insurance generally cost $100-200, so a good target amount to save would be $6,300. Polly Pennywise and Pam were ready to start saving for their vacation. If they could save $1000 a month they'd be ready to pay for their vacation in just over six months. But if they could only save $500 a month, it would take them a year.

"Nanny, this seems like a lot of money to save!"

"I know it seems very intimidating but here's what I suggest. Because I'm the one who wants the luxury hotel, how about I contribute more? If we need $1000 a month I'll contribute $800. That way you only have to save $200 a month, or $50 a week. That's just over seven dollars a day.

"Actually, by saving that much every day for 30 days, it would give you $210 a month. After six months of saving, you'd have an extra $60 to spend."

Six months would give Pam and Polly Pennywise lots of time to research and read about the history of Malta. Pam planned to speak to her Aunt Heather to find out if she could trace any of her relatives in Malta. It was going to be an amazing trip!

They also planned to take along a list of safety tips for travelling:

Safety Tips for Travelling

☺ Use a money belt under your clothing to carry cash, passport and credit cards. Keep only a small amount of cash in pockets or wallets. Don't carry large amounts of cash and don't flash your cash in public, since this could make you a target for theft.

☺ Always keep your passport locked in a hotel room safe with a personal code, or in a money belt on your person. Never leave your passport unattended or lying around in your room.

☺ Become familiar with security issues in the area you're visiting. Some city sectors considered high crime areas should be avoided, especially at night. Be alert for pickpockets, especially in airports and large malls. You may stand out when you're a tourist in another country and therefore be targeted.

☺ Consider carrying two wallets with you – one your real wallet, the other with things that look like credit cards, with perhaps a few dollars, but nothing of real value. If threatened, toss the worthless wallet with the petty cash in one direction and run the other way. It's a small price to get rid of a criminal. Never fight to keep your money or purse; it could cost you your life.

☺ Pay cash for an airline limousine to the airport. There've been cases of credit card fraud when using credit cards in this situation. Don't risk ruining your vacation.

About the Author

Joanne Shaw is a Certified Financial Planner. She specializes in helping families to reach their financial goals, over the long-term, through comprehensive financial and strategic planning. She has worked in the area of finance for over 16 years and in that time has seen many people confused and afraid regarding their finances.

Joanne was the executor for both her father and mother. When her father passed away her mother barely knew how to write a cheque. There are so many vulnerable people and in particular older women who aren't actively involved in the day-to-day finances of their own lives. Women still make less money than men. They have higher expenses in everything from haircuts to clothes, and they live longer than men. This means that the desperate need to educate people with regard to money and finance is of particular concern for girls and women.

The Polly Pennywise series of books has been written with this in mind, with the hope that all children will understand and gain control of their financial health from a young age. In a world where credit and debt are the norm it is hoped that these books will help to stay the mass destruction of people's finances by teaching the fundamentals of money management. We owe it to our children to educate them about these fundamentals.

Current books:

Polly Pennywise goes Grocery Shopping
Polly Pennywise buys a Car
Polly Pennywise takes a Vacation
Polly Pennywise gives to Charity

Future books:

Polly Pennywise buys a Home
Polly Pennywise does a Renovation
Polly Pennywise pays Taxes
Polly Pennywise does Investing
Polly Pennywise goes to School
Polly Pennywise and the Magic Number